GOD'S WORDS ARE SWEET MELODY IN OUR EARS AND RESTORE OUR SPIRIT.

INSPIRATIONAL SCRIPTURES AND WORDS OF GOD....

BY VICTORIA GRACE

... FROM SADNESS TO GLADNESS

THANKS AND ACKNOWLEDGMENTS

I would like to take this time to thank and acknowledge the following important people in my life. My husband Joe for his constant encouragement, and my daughters Davina and Danica as they serve as my inspirations. These two young ladies inspired me to keep my faith in the Lord Jesus Christ. As I looked at their innocent faces and watched them put their faith in Jesus Christ at a very young age, it inspired me to grow and strengthen my faith in God. Finding joy in every circumstance.

This book came about in my daily devotion and reading of the bible every day. God is righteousness, peace, and joy in the Holy Ghost. Hope is the life-spring of joy, and full of hope. When I look at my life...I am where I am, where Christ wants me to be. Amid turmoil and trouble...Christ is with me; I have inner peace...I have inner joy. In sadness and disappointment, through it all, Jesus Christ is guiding me, caring for me, and loving me. Christ is indeed all around me. Rejoice in the Lord always.

ABOUT THE AUTHOR

Victoria Grace is a dedicated and faithful servant of the Lord Jesus Christ, Sunday school teacher (children and adults), Homegroup Leader, Life Coach, Christian Motivational Speaker, author, educator, and Ladies' Group Facilitator. My experience in social services for twenty years has given me different perspectives on life and the world. In my free time, I like spending my time outdoors as I enjoy nature and photography, which are my hobbies. My writing derives from my everyday life experiences and is inspired by reading the words of God (Bible) everyday.

Through Jesus Christ, who gives me strength, I am able to face the reality of my past, lay everything down at the feet of Jesus. To forgive myself as the Lord has forgiven me. Throughout all my life's experiences, God is always there with me, loving me as it says in Jeremiah 29:11, "For I know the plans I have for you," declares the Lord, "plans to prosper you and not to harm you, plans to give you hope and a future."

PREFACE

Jonah 2:2 He said: "In my distress I called to the Lord, and he answered me. From deep in the realm of the dead, I called for help, and you listened to my cry.

God hears our cry for help, even though we have brought troubles upon ourselves. God is always there to save and rescue us from all troubles. It is the miracle of deliverance. Sometimes, we just want to find an escape. We will end up in a tragedy if God just lets go of us. But God is a loving God. When in distress, call upon God, and he will deliver us from all evil and peril.

THE JOY OF THE LORD IS OUR STRENGTH…..

Psalm 59:16 – 17: But I will sing of your strength, in the morning I will sing of your love; for you are my fortress, my refuge in times of trouble. You are my strength, I sing praise to you; you, God, are my fortress, my God on whom I can rely. Psalms 59, David cried out to God when he was in a depth of despair. God heard his cry, and he comforted him.

We live in a world where unfairness and injustice seem to triumph. The rich get richer, and the poor get poorer. When wrong seems right, and the darkness hovers us relentlessly. Standing up for what is right is a fight we battle each day. Giving up is sometimes the best, and succumbing to the lure of unrighteousness. Our eyes become a fountain of tears. Our hearts are heavily burdened with sadness and sorrow. God comforts us during our struggles and distress. Stand firm and trust in the Lord God Almighty. Through it all, we will discover God's everlasting love.

Colossians 4:6: Let your conversation be always full of grace, seasoned with salt, so that you may know how to answer everyone.

Are our words kind encouragement, wise counsel, and gentle comfort? Or are they like piercing swords that leave others bleeding.... With God's love and wisdom, we can create kind and gracious words that are music to our ears. They enliven our hearts and even our steps. Our faces glow by their instant effect, and energy and vitality are quickly restored.

Psalms 119:105: Your word is a lamp to guide my feet and a light for my path.

Each day brings joy and sadness, trials and tribulations. When we let God's words guide us, we will get through life's struggles… Our burden will be light, and he restores our spirit. Have faith in God; he controls everything that goes on in our lives. Keep smiling and keep loving. Our God is an awesome God.

2 Corinthians 4:18: "We fix our eyes not on what is seen, but on what is unseen, since what is seen is temporary, but what is unseen is eternal."

Our troubles should not diminish our faith; we should not resent our troubles; we should look at them as opportunities. They keep us from our pride and look beyond this brief life. After all, God is in control of everything.

Isaiah 41:10: So do not fear for I am with you. Do not be dismayed for I am your God. I will strengthen you and help you. I will uphold you with my righteous right hand.

We often question our life and our future. We also seem to compare ourselves with others. Sometimes life seems unfair to most of us. We feel as though we are dealt a wrong deck of cards, and our luck runs out. We cannot seem to be content with what we have. As we yearn more for what we want as opposed to what we need. We forget to be thankful and to be grateful for what we are blessed with. We feel defeated with many regrets. Why is it so? Are we really that destitute, desolate, and desperate about life? Is there a hope for humanity?

Yes, we have hope through Jesus Christ, our Lord and Savior. Let's look at our life through heaven's eyes. We will find that we are blessed more than we can imagine. Life itself is a blessing to us all. Let us then cherish it and be grateful for the life we have. It is a gift from heaven above, Life that is more precious than any treasures this world has to offer.

**Jeremiah 29:11: "For I know the plans I have for you,"
declares the Lord, plans to prosper you and NOT to harm you.
Plans to give you hope and a future."**

We often misunderstood the idea that God's plans for us will come out of the blue. Thus, we often do not know what God's plans are for our lives. God calls us and guides us when we are faced and immersed with challenges in the moment. As seen in the bible, God calls his people when they are in difficult situations. Obedience is the key to finding God's will and plan for us. We are often reluctant to follow God's command as it requires our full commitment. Fear has also become part of our disobedience; therefore, we need to fully trust God, as he is in control of everything. It is imperative that we obey when God calls and commands us to do something for his name and glory. To be obedient to God's commands, we need to posses' strong faith and believe that God is with us always.

Romans 12:12: Rejoice in our confident hope. Be patient in trouble, and keep on praying.

We often ask what the world is coming to; with all these changes happening around us, we often ask where God is in all of these. God never leaves us, but he allows things to happen in order for us to learn what is right and what is wrong. We say the world is corrupt, but we are part of this world. As Christians and followers of Jesus Christ, we need not look at the world in worldly passion but look at the world through heaven's eyes. With strong faith and with God's love – we can love the unlovable. After all, who are we to judge one another. We will miss God's presence and calling when we are focused on ourselves, what is going on around us, and what is good for us alone by disregarding what is more important. Love God and love others is God's greatest commandments to all. Love regardless and despite. We all fall short, and we all live an imperfect life.

1 John 4:16: We have come to know and have believed the love which God has for us. God is love, and the one who abides in love abides in God, and God abides in him.

We are in this world but not of this world.
We are with God, but we are not God.
To live a godly life, we are to be united with God.
God dwells within us, and His love shines through us.
When God is with us, it will manifest itself within us.
Others then will see God's love through us.
God alone can transform and renew one's mind and heart through Christ Jesus, our Lord and Savior.

Psalm 28:7: The Lord is my strength and my shield, my heart trusts in Him and He helps me.

Happiness is not guaranteed in life. We must make it happen for ourselves. Our ability to find humor and laughter in any given situation is a gift to give ourselves. Let's face it life is funny with its quirks and contradictions. To gain new perspectives to make others smile and laugh. Unlock our key to happiness with a sense of humor. Let's look for humor in everything, in every circumstance, in every situation. Laugh more and live a happy life.

Habakkuk 2:3: For the vision is yet for an appointed time, but at the end it shall speak, and not lie: though it tarry, wait for it; because it will surely come, it will not tarry.

Are we willing to sacrifice all and leave everything to serve a higher purpose and not for ourselves alone? We are here to follow this path set out before us and for others to do God's work and share God's love with all. Indeed, it is time to show the world the POWER of GOD!! The world will change radically in a positive and loving way. It is time to communicate our ideas and share our common goal and purpose, caring and loving one person at a time and the world beyond as we create a peaceful, harmonious, and prosperous new world. God's name will be glorified. We are the instruments of God to bring hope, love, and life to all mankind. Together, we are One, One Hope, One God. The time is now, and it's time to begin.

Titus 3:5: Not by works of righteousness which we have done, but according to his mercy he saved us, by the washing of regeneration, and renewing of the Holy Spirit.

Seeing through God's eyes…. God looks at individuals and sees their needs, and responds accordingly. Look at life through heaven's eyes. When we begin to see people as God does, we'll no longer look at them as enemies but as souls in need of grace. This is how Jesus could give His life for us. He saw our great need. When someone wrongs us, do not seek to retaliate, instead let us pray to understand the need behind the offender's actions.

Proverbs 3:5- 6: Do not depend on your own understanding. Seek his will in all you do, and he will show you which path to take.

If our integrity is in question. We must respond with grace and humbleness. Let our words be of truth without malice. Speak with honesty without manipulation to gain favor from others. Be wary of flattery as it is a form of manipulation, and it is a fleeting word without truth. In all our ways, let us acknowledge God, and He will direct our path. Let us not lean on our own understanding. With discernment, God gives us wisdom.

1 Corinthians 15:19: If in Christ we have hope in this life only, we are of all people most to be pitied.

Today is another day. We are blessed to be alive and well. So much is unknown about life…about the future. Today is what we have been given to enjoy, let us be thankful for the time we get to spend with God, with our loved ones, and with people we meet. New day, new opportunities, new challenges we face. Everything that is of today is a gift from God. All is designed according to God's plan for us today. Our response to negative messages we receive is our own responsibility. Don't let negativity dampen our spirit and prevent us from enjoying the blessings of today. Today is a gift, which is why it is called a "present."

Ecclesiastes 4:9-10: Two are better than one because they have a good return for their work: If one falls down, his friend can help him up. But pity the man who falls and has no one to help him up!

Today is a new day. New beginning. I decided to let go of things and people who took me for granted and hurt me. I want to live my life happily with people who matter to me, and I matter to them. We may never forget them; we also never regret knowing them. God is the only best friend we could ever have because He never leaves us nor forsake us. Let us then forgive, let go, and pray for those who wronged us. Everything happens for a reason…thus, we never let our past and regrets hinder us on the path to happiness.

Philippians 2:3-4: Do nothing from rivalry or conceit, but in humility count others more significant than yourselves. Let each of you look not only to his own interests but also to the interests of others.

Today, everyone seems to put his/her own needs first. We are often confused by evil and chaos; hence, we ignore God's direction. We often felt religious …and doing good deeds is enough. We wanted to maintain religious influence in our homes, to others, and to people we meet each day. We forget that religion does not save anyone. Do not think that good intentions are enough. Otherwise, we might think that we do not need instructions from God's Word. If we truly love God, we will have the desire to follow his law and know what we should do about it. Drawing closer to God and his word reminds us of what is right…what really matters.

1 John 4:7: Beloved, let us love one another, for love is from God, and whoever loves has been born of God and knows God.

To love and care for all mankind should be our heart's desire. Perhaps it is an illusion or hopeless desire. But God is always in control of all that we desire. May it be for the good of all that, in the end, we may find ourselves glorifying God, for we are created to glorify God. Let us then love one another as God is love. Let love be our guide in all that we do and speak. As we aspire to lead people, we need to be united. We are being tested with our faith in one another, and we are letting the darkness win. I am not perfect. I have more faults than any good in me. Each day, I just trust God that He will walk with me and give me eyes to see goodness and beauty in all that I see.

Galatians 6:9: "And let us not grow weary of doing good, for in due season we will reap, if we do not give up."

Timing is important. All the experiences we experienced are timed according to God's plan for us. The secret to having peace with God is to accept, discover, and appreciate God's perfect timing. When is there time for hating? We shouldn't hate people…. but hate the evil deeds. In addition, we should hate sins in our lives. Don't take life as a big irresponsible party…instead, take pleasure in what we do through God, and enjoy life as it is a gift from God. True enjoyment in life comes only as we follow God's guidelines for living. We will truly enjoy life when one take life each day as a gift from God, thanking God for it and serving him in it.

Isaiah 40:31: "But they who wait for the Lord shall renew their strength; they shall mount up with wings like eagles; they shall run and not be weary; they shall walk and not faint."

There are moments in our lives when someone makes us feel inferior and very small. How we respond to it and how we take it says a lot about ourselves and our characters. We do not need to act or treat them the same way we are treated. Response with gentleness and yet be assertive. Sometimes, making the other person feel bigger and better than you is a good response. There will be a day when the circumstances turn against them. Besides, God has the ultimate victory. It is better to play the role of a fool than to be a fool.

Romans 14:17-19: For the kingdom of God is not a matter of eating and drinking but of righteousness and peace and joy in the Holy Spirit. Whoever thus serves Christ is acceptable to God and approved by men. So then, let us pursue what makes for peace and for mutual upbuilding.

We do not know what the future holds; thus, we forget to rest in God's loving arms. We are often so preoccupied with our everyday burdens and cares that we miss completely the true meaning of peace. Our stubbornness and independence from God lead us to unnecessary chaos and turmoil. Instead of creating peace amongst our fellowmen, we create barriers and build a wall of hatred for one another. We may not understand each other, but we can still have peace as we work together for the betterment of all mankind. Peace is something we acquire through faith and trust in Christ, our Lord and Savior. May we all find peace and joy in the Holy Spirit.

Romans 12:2: Do not conform to the pattern of this world but be transformed by the renewing of your mind. Then you will be able to test and approve what God's will is–his good, pleasing, and perfect will.

The behavior and customs of this world are usually selfish and often corrupting. Our refusal to conform to the world must be deeper than just our behavior and customs. It must be firmly bound in our minds. We are to be transformed by the renewal of our minds. It is possible to avoid the world's ways and still be proud, covetous, arrogant, selfish, and stubborn. God has good, pleasing, and perfect plans for his people. He wants us to be new people with freshness of thought, alive to glorify him. Since God wants only what is best for us, he gave us his only Son, Jesus Christ, to make our new life possible. We should joyfully accept the newness of our being. Only when our minds are renewed by the new attitude Christ gives us are we truly transformed. If our character is like Christ, we can be sure our behavior will be pleasing to God.

Deuteronomy 31:6: Be strong and courageous. Do not fear or be in dread of them, for it is the Lord your God who goes with you. He will not leave you or forsake you.

Having the right attitude about God can help us deal with present injustices in this world. Prosperity is not always good, and adversity is not always bad. But God is always good, if we live as God wants us to, we will experience contentment through Christ Jesus.

Deuteronomy 13:4: It is the LORD your God you must follow, and him you must revere. Keep his commands and obey him; serve him and hold fast to him.

Following God one yes at a time. There are many obstacles and barriers that deter us from following God. One of the obstacles is PRIDE; we often let pride rule our hearts. We neglect to let the Holy Spirit govern our hearts and minds. We often do not recognize the will of God for us because of our pride. We are blinded by our ego, and we often think we are better than others. Following God should be easy if we obey and are willing to humble ourselves. Knowing that we are no better than others. God and God alone shaped this universe we call our own. Let us abide by God's word and hold on to His teaching.

Deuteronomy 28:66: Your life shall hang in doubt before you. Night and day you shall be in dread and have no assurance of your life.

DOUBTS

Our doubts lead us to unbelief....

The goal of every human should be to grow to be more mature every day. This is the process often called sanctification, where we seek to grow and become more mature. Goals sometimes are achieved, but many times, we fall short of our goals. It takes faith to grow spiritually. Many times, we have stumbling blocks or things that come up in our lives that keep us from growing. We all have some doubts in our life. Maybe we have doubted God. Maybe we have doubted that He is good. Maybe something in our lives has happened, and we just cannot make sense of our faith. Pray and meditate and allow God to strengthen us through the Holy Spirit. God gives us wisdom that surpasses all understanding.

Matthew 7:12: So whatever you wish that others would do to you, do also to them.

This Golden Rule seems to have been swept under a rug and is rarely used these days. We think more of what we can get rather than what we can give. Are we making a positive impact on our children and the people around us? To make an impact on someone's life; take the initiative to do something good to others, it is the foundation of goodness and mercy. The kind that God shows us every day. That will bring us happiness and joy.

1 Corinthians 13:13: And now these three remain: faith, hope and love. But the greatest of these is love.

When we fully understand God's love. It will reside in our hearts and minds. Reconditioning and renewing of mind will be easy and complete with God. We then can look at the world, ourselves, our lives, and others from different perspectives. There is love, grace, and hope. Hence, joy will follow you each day. But the greatest way to find joy is through love.

Revelation 4:1: After this, I looked, and there before me was a door standing open in heaven. And the voice I had first heard speaking to me like a trumpet said, "Come up here, and I will show you what must take place after this."

Here, we see the throne in heaven, a glimpse into Christ glory. God is orchestrating all the events. The earth is not spinning out of control. God will carry out his plans as Christ initiates the final battle against the evil one. Do not be frighten God is with us to the end. What a great promise from God that we can rely on.

Revelation 1:15: His feet were like bronze glowing in a furnace, and his voice was like the sound of rushing waters.

When we are faced with difficulties, remember Jesus walks with us with reassuring love. Always remember his deep love, and he cares for us. Jesus' love is pure and cleanses us from all impurity.

The rushing water is God's grace and promises unending joy as The Lord transforms our sadness into gladness.

PSALMS 139:1-5: Lord you have examined my heart and know everything about me. When far away, you know my thoughts. You chart the path ahead of me; you tell me where to stop and rest. Every moment you know where I am. You precede and follow me, and place your hand of blessing upon me.

God knows everything about us, but He loves us, nonetheless. God always with us through every situation and every trial --- protecting, loving, and guiding us. However, we don't let people know us completely because we are afraid they will discover something about us they won't like. But God knows us completely.

Each of us dreams and makes plans. We work hard to see those dreams and plans come true. To truly make the most of life, we must include God's plan in our plans. God alone knows what's best for us. As we make plans and dream dreams, tell God about them. God knows us completely.

Psalms 125:1: Those who trust in the Lord are as steady as the Mount Zion, unmoved by any circumstance.

In time of our need God is on our side. God will provide a way out, we need only to trust him. God never changes and will keep us steady and secure. Keeping our eyes on the Lord Jesus Christ will ultimately bring us unending joy.

Psalms 90:12: Teaches us to number our days, that we may gain a heart of wisdom.

Realizing that life is short helps us use the little time we have more wisely. It helps us concentrate on using our lives for eternal good, not just for the pleasure of the moment. Take time to number your days by asking; What do I want to see happen in my life before I die? What life step could I take toward that purpose today? It is easy to forget how short life really is.

Psalms 73:25-26: Whom have I in heaven but You? And besides You, I desire nothing on earth. My flesh and my heart may fail, But God is the strength of my heart and my portion forever.

God is the source of our daily needs and life itself. He wants us to understand the importance of giving Him the glory and honor. Let us worship God in all that we do and wherever we go.

So, I return to hope and praise for you, the God who saved me, who also gave me a purpose and told me what I needed to accomplish.

It has never been about me, as much as I want to think it is. It is all about your plan of eternal redemption, about your glory, about your work, about your kingdom and you are big enough to handle IT, the enemy, and my feebleness.

Is it about trusting Father God? Today, I know that I need you so much!

**Psalms 71:5-6: Sovereign Lord, I put my hope in you; I have trusted in you since I was young. I have relied on you all my life; you have protected me since the day I was born.
I will always praise you.**

Remembering God's lifetime of blessings will help us see the consistency of His grace throughout the years. It will help us trust God for the future. It also motivates us to share with others the benefits of following God. How great is the assurance that God is always with us at every step of our lives? Our obedience to God's will, it will help others to see God's grace, mercy, and love. May we live a life that is pleasing and acceptable to God? May we always speak love with kindness and compassion. Always loving and always caring as God loves and cares for us.

Psalms 46:1-3 1: God is our refuge and strength an ever-present help in trouble. 2 Therefore we will not fear, though the earth give way and the mountains fall into the heart of the sea, 3 though its waters roar and foam and the mountains quake with their surging.

We fear that the mountains and cities crumbling into the sea by a nuclear blast haunt us today. However, God assures us that even to the world's ends, we need not fear. Let us express a quiet confidence in God that can save us even in the face of utter destruction. God is not merely a temporary refuge, but he is our eternal refuge. God gives us the strength to face the uncertainties of life.

Psalms 16:9: Heart, body, and soul are filled with joy.

True joy is far deeper than happiness, joy can be felt even amid and in spite of one's troubles. Joy is based on God's presence within us. As we contemplate God's daily presence, we may find contentment and peace. Let us not base our life on circumstance but on God.

Psalm 107:8: Let them give thanks to the Lord for his unfailing love and his wonderful deeds for mankind,

Life presents so many challenges every day, whether at work, at home or just on a normal day. One thing is for sure: God is in control of everything. No matter what challenges we face, we can be confident that God is with us.

Life is a mystery, but God said abide in me, and I'll abide in you. Don't dwell in the past, live and enjoy the present, look forward to tomorrow. God is not yet finished shaping our tomorrow.

Psalm 37:4: Take delight in the Lord, and he will give you the desires of your heart.

What is happiness? Is it something we create or something we acquire? According to the bible, "happy are those who delight in the Lord." Therefore, abiding and obedience in God's words and commands give us eternal joy and happiness. We need not to create a happy lifestyle for ourselves. When we delight in the Lord, happiness comes naturally.

Psalm 32:11: Rejoice in the Lord and be glad, you righteous; sing, all you who are upright in heart!

To rejoice in the Lord always means to thank and give all glory to God in good times and in bad times. When our hearts are right with God, we can always sing for joy. We sometimes feel as though there is no hope when the going tough. Let us remember that God is in control of everything. Rejoice always and be glad that we are given another day, another chance to glorify God, and sing for joy.

Psalm 16:11: You make known to me the path of life; in your presence there is fullness of joy; at your right hand are pleasures forevermore.

There are moments in life when we are thrown into a troubled path. What we make of it is our own choice. We can choose to be happy as to come what may and make it better for us. Sometimes, what we want is not what God wants for us. To accept this reality is really freeing ourselves from sinful things and from temptations. We often overlook what we have been given, and we have tendency to take our blessings for granted. But God is good, and he always redeems us and restores our souls. Things/people we take for granted because they meant nothing to us. Unknowingly or knowingly, we hurt those people we took for granted. It is hard and it is hurtful to be taken for granted. We may or may not be blessings to them or to us; we never know. But one thing is for sure: we are always loved by the one who died for us on the cross, Jesus Christ. Sometimes, we are put in a place where we can discover ourselves and find who we are in God.

Proverbs 14:27: The fear of the LORD is a fountain of life, turning a man from the snares of death.

When we fear the Lord, we develop love. Love that is of God. We no longer fear life here on Earth. We are more concerned about life that we are going to have in heaven. Love God and love others. Be a fountain of life. We will also develop joy that is of God, unspeakable joy.

Proverbs 12:18: Reckless words pierce like a sword, but the tongue of the wise brings healing.

WORDS.... bring forth life and hope
WORDS... bring us down or kill our spirit.
WORDS ... only thing we must draw people in our heart.
WORDS... once spoken, we never get it back.
Let our WORDS be of kindness, compassion, love, and encouragement.
Let us speak WORDS of life, love, purity without malice.

Proverbs 4:23: "Above all else, guard your heart, for everything you do flows from it."

Give careful thought to the paths for our feet and be steadfast in all our ways. Guarding the heart really means our inner core, our thoughts, feelings, desires, will, and choices that make us who we are. Our mind reflects who we really are, not simply our actions or words. God examines our hearts, not simply our outward appearance and what we appear to be.

Psalms 139:23-24: Point out anything in me that offends you, and lead me along the path of everlasting life.

Every day of our lives, we are often confused and unclear about what God wants from us. We often think we are doing fine and all is well. However, if we ask God to search our inner being, God will find faults, flaws, and dark thoughts. We often pray for forgiveness, and God is so gracious in forgiving us. God knows our limitations as human beings incapable of perfection. Therefore, abiding and trusting God in all that we do is a must. God loves us so and wants the best for us.

Philippians 1:20: I eagerly expect and hope that I will in no way be ashamed but will have sufficient courage so that now as always Christ will be exalted in my body, whether by life or by death.

As a believer, life meant developing eternal values and telling others about Christ. Jesus Christ alone can help us see life from in eternal perspective. Our purpose is to live and speak boldly like Christ. Once we know our eternal purpose. We are free to serve---devoting our lives to what really counts without fear of dying. Hence, we can confidently say that death is merely going to see Christ face to face. When we are not ready to die, we are not ready to live.

Philippians 1:9: And this I pray, that your love may abound yet more and more in knowledge and in all judgment;

When believers draw upon Christ's love, all Christians are part of God's family. And we all share the equal opportunity in the transforming power of God's love. There are times when we longed to see a friend with whom we share fond memories. We often feel deep love for our fellow Christian friends and strangers alike. Let Christ's love motivate us to love others, and feel free to express that love.

Philippians 4:13: I can do everything God asks me to with help of Christ who gives me strength and power.

True contentment lies in our perspectives, our priorities, and our source of power. We should draw near to God when we feel empty inside. And look at our lives through heaven's eyes.

Philippians 4:4-5: Rejoice in the Lord always. I will say it again: Rejoice! 5 Let your gentleness be evident to all.

Ultimate joy comes from Christ dwelling within us. Our inner attitude does not have to reflect our outward circumstances. Be full of Christ's joy no matter what happens. It is easy to get discouraged about unpleasant circumstances and unimportant events. If we haven't been joyful lately, perhaps we are not looking at life from the right perspective. Be joyful always, the Lord is our strength and joy.

Philippians 4:13: I can do all things through him who strengthens me.

We all walk different paths in life…we all have struggles along the way. We trip, we fall, and we get hurt. But, as long as we include God throughout our journey of life, all things will become possible and new. In the end, what we make of our life's experiences is what makes us. We have everything we need…all we must do is believe.

Philemon 1:7: Your love has given me great joy and encouragement, because you, brother, have refreshed the hearts of the Lord's people.

Loving and forgiving our fellow believers brings life and renews our spirits. We can choose to love or not to love others, but what would that accomplish? In the end, it is not about you, me, or them….it is all about God. Show kindness whenever we can, whenever possible. Love always, no matter the circumstance.

Nehemiah 1:11: Lord, let your ear be attentive to the prayer of this your servant and to the prayer of your servants who delight in revering your name. Give your servant success today by granting him favor in the presence of this man."

Each of us is unique and capable of serving God no matter what our position is. Be prepared and look for the right opportunity to tell others about God's love. We can use our present positions to serve God. How many of our actions today will be done with the purpose of pleasing God?

Matthew 13:44: "The kingdom of heaven is like treasure hidden in a field. When a man found it, he hid it again, and then in his joy went and sold all he had and bought that field.

The Kingdom of Heaven is more valuable than anything else we can have, so a person must be willing to give up everything to obtain it. When we find a treasure in heaven, as Christ said, leave everything behind and follow me. Are we willing to give up everything, follow Christ, and store treasures in Heaven?

They are those days when everything seems to be falling apart. When the only thing is hope for the best. Today is one of those days. I must trust God to keep it together for me. God is good, and I am thankful.

A Simple Sinner's Prayer ("For all have sinned and fall short of the glory of God" Romans 3:23)

Dear Heavenly Father, I come to you in the name of Jesus Christ. I acknowledge to You that I am a sinner, and I am sorry for my sins and the life that I have lived; I need your forgiveness.

I believe that your only Son, Jesus Christ, shed His precious blood on the cross at Calvary and died for my sins, and I am now willing to repent, confess, and turn from my sin. You said in the bible that if I confess the Lord our God and believe in my heart that God raised Jesus from the dead, I shall be saved.

I confess Jesus Christ as my Lord and my Saviour. With my heart, I believe that God raised Jesus from the dead. At this very moment, I accept Jesus Christ as my own personal Savior, and according to His Word, I am saved. Amen.

www.ingramcontent.com/pod-product-compliance
Lightning Source LLC
Chambersburg PA
CBHW050302120526
44590CB00016B/2457